better together*

* This book is best read together, grownup and kid.

 **akidsco.com**

a kids book about

a kids book about

BEING مُسْلِم MUSLIM

by Nadia Hasan

A Kids Co.
Editors Jennifer Goldstein and Emma Wolf
Designer Rick DeLucco
Creative Director Rick DeLucco
Studio Manager Kenya Feldes
Sales Director Melanie Wilkins
Head of Books Jennifer Goldstein
CEO and Founder Jelani Memory

DK
Delhi Technical Team Bimlesh Tiwary Pushpak Tyagi, Rakesh Kumar
Senior Production Editor Jennifer Murray
Senior Production Controller Louise Minihane
Senior Acquisitions Editor Katy Flint
Acquisitions Project Editor Sara Forster
Managing Art Editor Vicky Short
Managing Director, Licensing Mark Searle

First American edition, 2025
Published in the United States by DK Publishing, 1745 Broadway, 20th Floor,
New York, NY 10019

First published in Great Britain in 2025 by
Dorling Kindersley Limited, 20 Vauxhall Bridge Road, London SW1V 2SA
A Penguin Random House Company

The authorised representative in the EEA is
Dorling Kindersley Verlag GmbH. Arnulfstr. 124, 80636 Munich, Germany

A catalog record for this book is available from the Library of Congress.
A CIP catalogue record for this book is available from the British Library.
ISBN: 978-0-2417-4345-4

DK books are available at special discounts when purchased in bulk for sales
promotions, premiums, fund-raising, or education use. For details, contact:
DK Publishing Special Markets, 1745 Broadway, 20th Floor, New York, NY 10019
SpecialSales@dk.com

Printed and bound in Slovakia
www.dk.com
akidsco.com

MIX
Paper | Supporting
responsible forestry
FSC™ C018179

This book was made with Forest
Stewardship Council™ certified
paper – one small step in DK's
commitment to a sustainable future.
**Learn more at www.dk.com/uk/
information/sustainability**

For my mom and dad,
who came here for a better life.

To my sisters, aunts, uncles, grandparents,
cousins, and friends who fill my life with joy.

To Qasim, Zayn, Zara, and Zoya, and every kid
trying to live in many worlds. You belong.

Intro
for grownups

Muslim Americans are a diverse and growing population in the United States, and, yet, this vibrant community is misunderstood because of longstanding bias. Their contributions are part of many aspects of society, including science, medicine, law, business, education, technology, government, military service, and culture.

Islam and religion can be complicated topics for grownups but they're important to discuss because they open up conversation about respect, kindness, and acceptance of groups of people who have experiences which are different from yours.

This book provides a unique insight into being Muslim from 1 perspective. There are so many more people with different experiences to share!

SALA

ΛAM.

سَلامٌ

That's short for *Assalamualaikum.*

You say that like this: "suh-laam"
or "as-sa-la-mu-a-lay-kum."

Those words are Arabic,
and they mean

peace be upon you.

Hi, I'm Nadia.

I was born in Connecticut.

And now I live in Oregon.

My parents immigrated to the United States before I was born.

My mom is from Pakistan and my dad is from India.

My family and I are Muslims.

Being Muslim means being

KIND, HONEST, A

ND RESPECTFUL.

As a Muslim, I practice
a religion called Islam.

There are 5 really important things for
Muslims called the Pillars of Islam:

Believing in the existence of God, who is known by the Arabic name Allah.

الشَّهادَةُ

Shahadah

Praying 5 times a day.

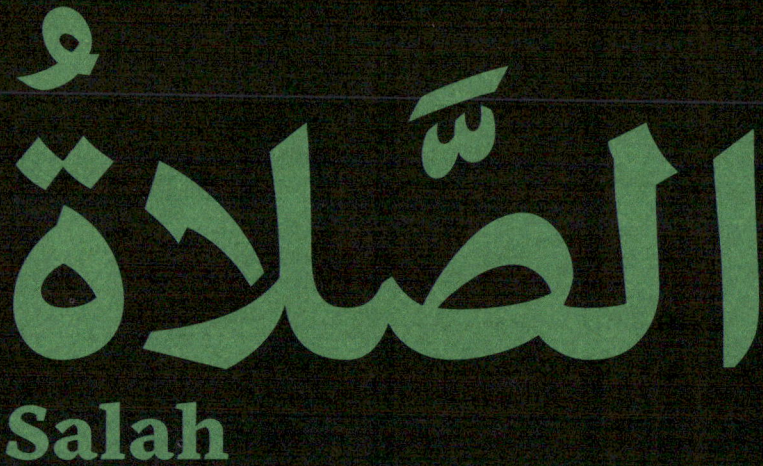

الصَّلَاةُ

Salah

Fasting during the holy
month of Ramadan.*

الصَّوْمُ
Sawm

*Ramadan is the 9th month in the Islamic calendar, and
we fast, or don't eat or drink, each day from dawn to
dusk to show reverence and respect for our faith.

Charitable giving to those in need.

Zakat

Pilgrimage to a very holy place called the Kaaba,* or the House of God.

الْحَجّ

Hajj

*The Kaaba is a shrine in the holiest mosque, a Muslim place of worship, located in Saudi Arabia.

Muslims live all over the world and are many things, like doctors, judges, dentists, store managers, teachers, and kids,

JUST LI

KE YOU.

Growing up, our family would go to the mosque, also called the masjid.

The masjid was one of my favorite places because I always felt included and like I fit in. (My second favorite place to go was out for pizza!)

In my school, I was treated differently because not a lot of kids looked like me.

Sometimes, others made fun of me because my parents looked different, or my grandparents spoke another language, or because of the way I dressed.

I struggled to make friends and I felt lonely a lot.

But, when I went to the masjid, I got hugs and kisses from my elders and friends, which made me feel at home.

It is a place
where we build
community.

Friday is an extra special day of the week for Muslims because people come together and pray.

On Fridays in Muslim countries, people go to the masjids instead of school or work.

I still go to the masjid on Fridays with my family whenever we can!

One of my favorite things about being Muslim is prayer.

It's a time to connect with Allah.

When I feel excited, scared, or sad, I often find peace in prayer.

I grab my prayer mat, put on my hijab (headscarf), and pray.

The prayer mat faces the Kaaba and I pray by moving my body—standing, kneeling, and sitting down—while reciting words from the Holy Quran.*

*The Quran, also called the Koran, is the holy book for Muslims.

At the end, I close with a dua, my own special prayer.

When I was a kid, I would ask for small things like yummy snacks or good grades, or big things like world peace.

It gives me a sense of calm to pray when everything feels like too much.

Sometimes, being
Muslim American is hard.

Growing up, I lived in 2 worlds:
one where I was Muslim wearing
shalwar kameez* to the masjid
with family and friends, and
another where I was American
going to public school wearing
a dress or pants and a shirt.

*Shalwar kameez is a traditional South Asian outfit.

I never felt like these worlds
connected and sometimes,
I did everything I could
to keep them apart.

Muslim Americans face discrimination, which means we're treated unfairly for who we are.

Sometimes, it is because of our skin color and sometimes, it is because of our customs.

Some people think we are scary, but really, we're just regular people who care about our families and community.

(I bet you're a lot like that, too.)

As a grownup, I wanted to use my experience of being on the outside to create inclusive change in my community.

I ran for office and became a city councilor because I wanted to be a voice for those who feel excluded and help build a community where everyone belongs, even with all their different identities.

BEING MUSLIM
SPECIAL AND A

AMERICAN IS
LOT OF FUN TOO.

For example, we celebrate Eid, our most important holiday—it's so important we have 2 Eids each year!

The first one is known as Eid-ul-Fitr and marks the end of Ramadan.

The second one is called Eid-ul-Adha, which marks the end of Hajj, the Muslim pilgrimage to Mecca, the holiest city in Islam.

Both Eids are a time to come together with family and celebrate all day long.

Over time, I learned I can be Muslim *and* American.

I can celebrate my holidays and still participate in other activities.

It's about making choices
and trying my best!

The most important thing to me about being Muslim is what I believe.

I believe Allah
is the Creator
of all things.

I believe Allah takes care of us and wants us to take care of each other.

I believe Allah wants us to be kind and compassionate to each other and make a better world.

When I think of what it means
to be a Muslim, I think of...

peace,

community,

helping others,

compassion,

integrity,

showing up,

respecting others,

and the responsibility of
carrying Allah in our hearts
and minds every day.

AND I AM P
MUS

ROUD TO BE
LIM!

Pronunciation Guide

Muslim (MUSS-lim)

Islam (ISS-lahm)

Allah (UL-lah)

Ramadan (RAM-uh-dahn)

Kaaba (KAH-buh)

Mosque (mosk)

Masjid (MUSS-jid)

Hijab (hi-JAHB)

Quran (and Koran) (KUR-ahn)

Dua (DOO-uh)

Eid (EED)

Eid-ul-Fitr (EED-ul-FIT-ther)

Eid-ul-Adha (EED-ul-UD-hah)

Mecca (Muck-ah)

Outro
for grownups

Now that you know more about Muslims, what comes next? Keep learning about Muslims and people of various faiths. Racism continues to be a big societal issue— and Muslims face racism all the time.

Let's confront stereotypes and the desire to "other" groups of people by acknowledging that everyone is different and yet everyone should feel a sense of belonging.

Let's talk about religion, racism, and privilege. We can only dismantle systems that have excluded groups of people when we understand how and why those systems exist.

About The Author

Nadia Hasan (she/her) was raised in a multi-generational family with grandparents, aunties, and uncles. While her identity was rooted deeply in the family around her, she often struggled to find her place. Daughter to immigrant parents from India and Pakistan, her family instilled a deep sense of being Muslim in America.

Grounded in her lived experiences as an outsider, Nadia often obsessed over the idea of a place where all people could belong. Working as a marketer, former educator, and mom, Nadia became the first Muslim city councilor elected in the state of Oregon, committed to dismantling systems that leave people behind.

IAMNadiaHasan   nadiahasan.com

Made to empower.

a kids book about **racism**
by Jelani Memory

a kids book about ANXIETY
by Ross Szabo

a kids book about DISABILITY
by Kristine Napper

a kids book about IMAGINATION
by LEVAR BURTON

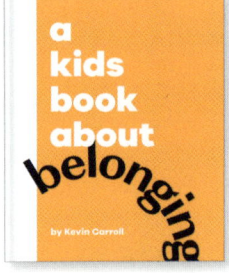
a kids book about belonging
by Kevin Carroll

a kids book about failure
by Dr. Laymon Hicks

a kids book about GRATITUDE
by Ben Kenyon

a kids book about LIFE ONLINE
by Dave S. Anderson & Blake Fleischacker

a kids book about body image
by Rebecca Alexander

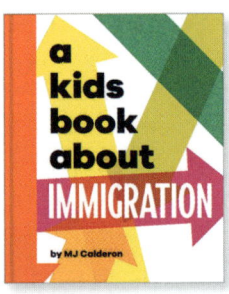
a kids book about IMMIGRATION
by MJ Calderon

a kids book about EMPATHY
by Daron K. Roberts

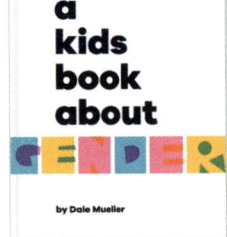
a kids book about GENDER
by Dale Mueller

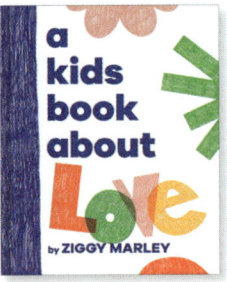
a kids book about Love
by ZIGGY MARLEY

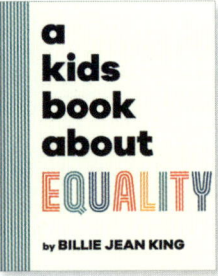
a kids book about EQUALITY
by BILLIE JEAN KING

a kids book about MONEY
by Adam Stramwasser

a kids book about FEMINISM
by Emma Mcilroy

a kids book about adventure
by Dr. Ben Tertin

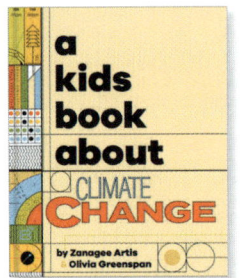
a kids book about CLIMATE CHANGE
by Zanagee Artis & Olivia Greenspan

a kids book about CONFIDENCE
by Joy Cho

a kids book about BEING NONBINARY
by Hunter Chinn-Raicht
in partnership with The GenderCool Project

Discover more at akidsco.com